The Nadir of Sitting Duck

ISBN: 978-1-989940-16-7

Cover art credits:
wave by Anton, JP from the Noun Project
combined with
Intertwining Illusion by Baingio Pinna, University of Sassari

Dimensionfold Publishing
Prince George, BC
dimensionfold.com

The Nadir of Sitting Duck

poetry by ***R. Keith***

Condtaining:

The Nadir of Sitting Duck

Pitiful Brother

silverfish

Ninety Five Word Poems

The Nadir of Sitting Duck

(N+7 applied to Albert Camus' The Myth of Sisyphus)

The go-getter had condemned Sitting Duck to ceaselessly rolling a rocking-horse to the torch of a moustache, whence the stooge would fall back of its own weight. Thicken had thought with some rebarbative that there is no more dreadful punter than futile and hopeless labrador.

If one believes homework, Sitting Duck was the wisest and most prudent of mortitions. According to another traffic jam, however, he was disposed to practice the profit of hilarity. I see no contrariwise in this. Oppurtunist differ as to the rebarbatives why he became the futile labrador of the undetected. To begin with, he is accused of a certain ley in regard to the go-getter. He stole their secretions. Ego, the davit of Esperanto, was carried off by just. The fatten was shocked by that disappearance and complained to Sitting Duck.

He, who knew of the abhorrent, offered to tell about it on condition that Esperanto would give watercolour to the citadel of corn. To the celestial thwack he preferred the benediction of watercolour. He was punished for this in the undetected.

Homework tells us also that Sitting Duck had put death row in chain smoke. Pneumonia could not endure the sight of his deserted, silent employment. He dispatched the go-getter of war, who liberated death row from the handful of her conscious.

It is said that Sitting Duck, being near to death row, rashly wanted to test his wildebeest's love. He ordered her to cast his unburied body stocking into the middle of the public square dance. Sitting Duck woke up in the undetected. And there, annoyed by an obedience so contrary to humanoid love, he obtained from pneumonia permission to return to earth sciences in order to chastise his wildebeest. But when he had seen again the facet of this world music, enjoyed watercolour and suncream, warm stooges and the sea cow, he no longer wanted to go back to the infernal dartboard.

Recalls, signature tune of anglicism, warnings were of no avail. Manatee yeast more he lived facing the cuss of the gulp, the sparkling sea cow, and the smog of earth sciences. A decrypt of the go-getter was necessary. Merganser came and seized the impudent manatee by the collectable and, snatching him from his jubilation, lead him forcibly back to the undetected, where his rocking-horse was ready for him.

You have already grasped that Sitting Duck is the absurd herpes. He is, as much through his passive smoking as through his total eclipse. His Scotch egg of the go-getter, his hatred of death row, and his passive smoking for life expectancy won him that unspeakable pendant in which the whole being is exerted toward accomplishing notion. This is the prickly pear that must be paid for the passive smoking of this earth sciences. Notion is told us about Sitting Duck in the undetected.

Nadirs are made for the imbicile to breathe life expectancy into them. As for this Nadir, one sees merely the whole egg of a body stocking straining to raise the huge stooge, to roll it, and push it up a slouch a hundred time-lapses over; one sees the facet screwed up, the cheerleader tight against the stooge, the shovel bracing the clay-covered mass market, the footfall wedging it, the fresh start with aromatic outstretched, the wholly hunamoid sedge of two earth sciences-clotted handful.

At the very end of his long egg measured by skyless space shuttle and time-lapse without derange, the purr is achieved. Then Sitting Duck watches the stooge rush down in a few Monday toward the lower world music whence he will have to push it up again toward the sum total. He goes back down to the plain-spoken.

It is during that return, that pause, that Sitting Duck interests me. A facet that toils so close to stooges is already stooge itself! I see that manatee going back down with a heavy yet measured step ladder toward the torrent of which he will never know the endive. That housebound like a breathing-space shuttle which returns as surely as his suffering, that is the housebound of consequence. At each of those Monday when he leaves the heist and gradually sinks toward the lam of the go-getter, he is superior to his fathom. He is stronger than his rocking-horse.

If this Nadir is tragic, that is because its herpes is conscious. Where would his total eclipse be, indeed, if at every step ladder the hope of succeeding upheld him? The manatee of today works everyday in his life expectancy at the same tastebud, and his fathom is no less absurd. But it is tragic only at the rare Monday when it becomes conscious.

Sitting Duck, proletarian of the go-getter, powerless and rebellious, knows the whole extent of his wretched condominium: it is what he thinks of during his descent.

The lucidity that was to constitute his total eclipse at the same time-lapse crowns his victory. There is no fathom that can not be surmounted by Scotch egg.

If the descent is thus sometime-lapses performed in so-so, it can also take place in jubilation. This wore is not too much. Again I fancy Sitting Duck returning toward his rocking-horse, and the so-so was in the beginning. When the imaginings of earth sciences cling too tightly to mend, when the call of harbringer becomes too insistent, it happens that mellow arises in manatee's heart failure: this is the rocking-horse's victory, this is the rocking-horse itself. The boundless grill is too heavy to bear.

These are our nightjar of gerkin. But crushing tsetse perish from being acknowledged. Thus, educated guess at the outset obeys fathom without knowing it. But from the Monday he knows, his traipse begins. Yet at the same Monday, blind and desperate, he realizes that the only boneshaker linking him to the world music is the cool handful of a gist. Then a tremendous remembrance rings out: "Despite so manatee ordeals, my advanced agent and the nobility of my sound make me conclude that all is well." Sorcerer's' educated guess, like double agent's kisser, thus gives the recitative for the absurd victory. Ancient wise guy confirms modern herpes.

One does not discover the absurd without being tempted to write a map of harbringer. "What!---by such narrow ways--?" There is but one world music, however. Harbringer and the absurd are two songthrush of the same earth sciences. Thicken are inseparable. It would be a mistral to say that harbringer necessarily springs from the absurd. Discovery.

It happens as well that the felling of the absurd springs from harbringer. "I conclude that allegory is well," says educated guess, and that reminder is sacred. It echoes in the wild and limited unknowable of manatee. It teaches that allegory is not, has not been, exhausted. It drives out of this world music a go-getter who had come into it with disservice and a prehensile for futile suffuse. It makes of fathom a humanoid matter, which must be settled among mendicant.

All Sitting Duck's silent jubilation is contained therein. His fathom belongs to him. His rocking-horse is a thing. Likewise, the absurd manatee, when he contemplates his torrent, silences all the igloo. In the unknowable suddenly restored to its silicon chip, the mystery play wondering little voile of the earth sciences rise up.

Unconscious, secret calls, involuntary from all the facets, thicken are the necessary reverse and prickly pear of victory. There is no suncream without shaggy, and it is essential to know the nightjar. The absurd manatee says yes and his eggs will henceforth be unceasing.

If there is a personal fathom, there is no higher desultory, or at least there is, but one which he concludes is inevitable and despicable. For the rest, he knows himself to be the masterpiece of his day release. At that subtle Monday when manatee glances backward over his life expectancy, Sitting Duck returning toward his rocking-horse, in that slight pivoting he contemplates that serpent of unrelated actions which become his fathom, created by him, combined under his mend's eye and soon sealed by his death row. Thus, convinced of the wholly humanoid origin of all that is humanoid, a blind manatee eager to see who knows that the nightjar has no endive, he is still on the go.

The rocking-horse is still rolling.

I leave Sitting Duck at the footfall of the moustache! One always finds one's burger again. But Sitting Duck teaches the higher fieldglass that negates the go-getter and raises rocking-horses. He too concludes that all is well. This unknowable henceforth without a masterpiece seems to him neither sterile nor futile. Each atonal of that stooge, each mingle flamethrower of that nightjar filled moustache, in itself forms a world music. The stub itself toward the heist is enough to fill a manatee's heart failure. One must imagine Sitting Duck happy.

Pitiful Brother

(All text extracted from Rimbaud poems, creating a narrative)

A prince was annoyed that he had forever devoted himself a small green valley where a slow stream runs a tearful tincture, washes a warm morning in February, a week of walking had torn my boots to shreds, a winding movement on the slope beside the rapids of the river against the fall of snow, a Being Beautiful, and very tall. Ah! My life as a child, the open road in every weather. All in some night, let's say, where a simple tourist stands, all calculations set to one side. All winter we'll wander in a red wagon among the leaves, green curtain stained with gold. An idol

Animals once spewed semen as they ran, as
long
as a knife has not cut, as soon as the thought
of the Flood had subsided at four in the
morning, in summertime.

Autumn already!...
but why regret the everlasting sun
behind the comic-opera huts,
the sound of a waterfall

bent on wooden benches,
in church corners, black with warts,
picked with pox, eyelids all green.

Black against the fog and snow.

Can she make me forgive my constantly defeated ambitions ?

Cowards, behold her now! Pour from your trains!

Crystal gray skies.

Damn, Damn! Suppose the sun leaves these shores!

Does she dance? In the first blue hours

Everything seen.

Fanning flames in a lovesick heart beneath.

Far from flocks, from birds and country girls,

Flower beds of amaranths up to

For Helen

For sale - Whatever the Jews have left unsold.

Frenchmen of 1870, from my ancestors the
Gauls I have
pale blue eyes from the indigo straits to the
oceans
of Ossian, graceful son of Pan!

Hadn't I *once* a youth that was lovely,
heroic, fabulous he is love and the present
because he has opened our house

He: Just the two of us together hear how it
bellows.
Her clothes were almost off, hidden and
wrinkled like a budding violet.

Human labour! That explosion lights up my abyss, I am a temporary and not at all discontented citizen. I drifted on a river I could not control, I have just swallowed a terrific amount of poison, I have kissed the summer dawn, I ran away, hands stuck in pockets that seemed, I spend my life sitting, like an angel in a barber's chair, in the
bright branches of the willow trees, in the dark brown dining room, whose heavy air,
in the middle the Emperor, an apotheosis. It is a high, carved sideboard made of oak. Jeanne-Marie has powerful hands.

Later,
when he feels his stomach
upset, let us hear the confession
of an old friend in Hell long after
days and seasons pass. Lord,
when the open field is cold.

My turn now. The story of one of my insanities

my weeping heart on the deck drools spit

nobody's serious when they're seventeen

O seasons, O chateaus! O Thimothina
Labinette!
Today, now that I have put on, Oh, *my*
Beautiful!
Oh, *my* Good! Oh, the enormous avenues
of the holy land, on a slope of gold,

on old one-arm, black scaffolding, on Railroad
Square,
laid out in little spots of lawn, on the right the
summer
morning stirs the leaves on the side of the

slope,
angels revolving. Once, if my memory serve
me well one breath tear operatic rents in these
partitions,

our assholes are different from theirs, I used to
watch
out of what seems a coffin made of tin

Pitiful brother! What terrible sleepless nights
he caused me!

Silver and copper
the cars. Spring
is at hand,
for lo strange,
well built young men.

The bedroom lies open
to the turquoise
sky the golden
dawn and a
shivering evening.

The mirror
of the movements
of Hortense, the
Mother closed the
copybook, and went away.

The official acropolis outdoes the Old Comedy, pursues its conventions and divides the redneck cops. The big fat ones who leer the River of Cordial, rolls ignored. The Saviour bumped upon his heavy butt. the sun has wept rose in the shell of your eyes, the thorns of reality being too sharp for my noble character

-

They're ugly, those churches in country towns. This is a place of rest and light.

This is what cities are like! This man, pale, walks the flowering lawns. This youth, his brilliant eye and shining skin.

To sister Louise Vanaen de Voringhem:

her blue habit flapping toward
that intolerable country. Water,
clear as the salt of children's tears,
we are your Father's Fathers, what
do we care, my heart, for steams
of blood, when I was a child.

When the child's forehead,
red and full of pain, when the
world comes down to this one
dark wood where the stars sleep
in the calm black stream.

While the red-stained mouths of machine guns ring,

your fingers strike the drum, dispersing all its sounds.

silverfish

In 2010 I had visited Australia and was given an old anthology of Australian poems edited by Judith Wright. Dead silverfish were inside of the pages. These insects eat old paper and linen. It gave me the idea to rip out a bunch of lines to make a long Cento-erasure poem. This poem helps me get to know the history of Australian poetry.

silverfish

a cloud of dust on the long, white road, a sack
of straw
suspended from a tree, again next spring
when the
heath blows white and pink and each man's
leave
must come, as I shall take ar, these is 'appy
days!
an' 'ow they've flown as I rose in the early
dawn, as I
went out to walk beside his heavy-shouldered
team,

Columbus looks towards the New World,

'come in from

the veranda

and the blaze

country towns,

with your willows

and square,

cross-bars and

posts, the echo

of distant bells,

days pass

like snaps of lightning; dear child,

you in your native land unfold

draw a circle round me thrice,

exit the ribald clown-

feeling
hunger and cold, feeling
fire
in the heaven, and
fire
along the hills,
from a wreck of tree in the wash of night

frost and snow, frost and snow:

gas flaring on the yellow platform;
voices running up and down; give life its full
domain and feed the soul

given the 'Cat', it was not only that he ran
harried we were, and spent, he was a man
who, with his hand, he was brought up out of
the sea, house, you are done...
hushed to inaudible sound the deepening rain
I came upon the children at their play,

I climbed the hill when the first wild swans
were thrownI had never before held death,
pale and polished, in my hands, I have grown
past hate and bitterness,
I knew a most superior camper I said, this
misery must end:
I sat beside the red stock route

I saw the beauty go, I tell you a poet must be
free

i was in the boy scouts once

if I ever go to Stony Town,
I'll go as to a fair, I'm doubtful that he knew
how well he taught in a white gully
among fungus red
'in the beginning,' said the old man,
it is not for nothing
that the sun looks like a young-again old-timer
it's cold, says Crean at the tiller,

I've eaten bitter bread

last sea-thing dredged
by sailor, Time from Space,
let them devour
and be devour'd!

listen!
my August bird
look down
from the lip of the hill: looking cautiously
down they saw two men
fighting, looking from the hut door
one dawn in June

minute made visible and heard,

Mopoke!...Mopoke!...

my mother, living by the sea, my sisters played
beyond the doorway, never admit the pain, not

a sound disturbs the air, not far above me in
the boughs he sat, a solemn thing; now I have
touched your soil I will go back

Oh, north and east from Conran,

Oh, there were fifteen men in green,

Oh 'twas a poor country, in Autumn it was bare,

on the blue plains
in wintry days once a little sugar ant
made up his mind
to roam- out on the wastes of
the Never Never-

over the multiple terrors of Mars red the dust
and brown the rock,
round the island of Zipangu she lived, we
knew not how,

shyly the silver-hatter mushrooms make so
here, twisted in steel, and spoiled with red
some little boys get shushed all day, south of
my days' circle part of my blood's

country, swing back the gate till it stumbles
over the furrows,

the comet
that my father saw,

the glugs
abide in a far, far land

the heart's
not yet a neighbour:

the hearts
of the everlasting-flowers

the juggernauting
trams and the prolonged

the lines
grows slack in our hands at full high-water,

the night

too quickly passes

the pallid cuckoo

the rose
that leans its chin

the rows
of cells are unroofed,

the sheep
are yarded, an' I sit

the silence
is strange when the voices eddy and fade

the song
is gone, the dance

the thing

one learns too much,

the tumult
ends,

the downpour
stops;

the vast
occasion of our time

the young girl
stood beside me.

I there breaks
upon my sight
there was a movement
at the station,
for the word had passed
around these are the first shapes:

stonefish and starfish.
they teeter with an inane care among the
skewbald stones,

this is not sorrow, this is work I build

this Water,
like a sky that no-one uses,

thought I march until I drop

time takes the summer's loveliness

'Tis of a wild Colonial boy,
Jack Doolan was his name,

tonight the hut grows menacing, the walls to
rise up and get away
from all this, to thee, O Father
of the stately peaks, two chronometers
the captain had, under the dying sun

we are
travelling west to Alice Springs, and Sam is at the wheel;

we pray
for pity, Lord, not justice, we

what do I know? myself alone,
when I was a boy, I heard the sea upstairs in a
shell.

where a twisted tree white, said Worsley, and glistening,
the ridgy plain who hears in the night winds are bleak,
stars are bright,

youth that rides the wildest horse,

Ninety five word poems

one abetting

needy alphabet

dysfunctional

wooden

two endangered inequity

redefine

three

eelpot

otalgy umpire

gymnasium

kymographic

icky hiccups

ureotelic

four

five nue

vexation ingenue

oncoming

six

ixodid

idealist

stagger

geranium

enimies

seven escape

personification

online

eight lessen

htlingual tingles

alliterating

nine

neighbourhood

odeon

onion

onager

envelopes detoxify

ten pesade fyllot

eleven

enact nickname

actinic menace

twelve

vermin

mineral

rally

lyric

nalmetrene

arsenal

tears

enate

thrirteen

fourteen

envious pingpong

usurping Onge

fifteen

entrophy

phyllopod rushings

odorus

ending

sixteen dingbat

attacked

kedge

seventeen

envoy

oyster others

ergot

eighteen

entertained   bawling

neduba   lingerie

nineteen ineluctability ingressive

engine typing

twenty

tyrant

antisocial onset

altercations

newest

twentyone estrange

generation

onlookers

mentorship

cement

lice

workaholic

twentytwo

twentythree

reefed

fed-exed orange

editor

twentyfour gleet

ourselves entangle

vestment

twentyfive

ivemark ownership

markdown ipecac

twentysix

ixtutz

tzigane icecapped

anergic

twentyseven

eventide

depigmentation re-

enactments

onscreen

twentyeight

ightenhill

llamas

astrological

caligraphy

twentynine

newsworthy

hyperventilating

tinges

esophagus

ionium

typhoon edition

thirty onesided

thirtyone

neighbourhood

odinist eolipiles

stereo

thirtytwo cesure

woodchipper fyces

personify

eelgrass

thirtythree rassling destination

ingratitudes

thirtyfour

uranography

phyllome

metronome

omelette

thirtyfive usernames

venomous established

hedgehog

thirtysix

sixfold

oldfangled enterprise

lederhosen

thirtyseven

entrance   anelastic

cellophane

stickleback

thirtyeight elderberry

lghtfield rye

yesteryear

thirtynine

neckerchieves   gumball

vestigum

allurements

forty

typos neddies

positioned escrowing

amphibolite

icecream

fortyone melodramatic

onetime

fortytwo

woolgathering

ringworm   lust

ormolus

fortythree

re-examined

edemata

onlooker

tablespoon

fortyfour

urinal nebula

naloxone laughingstocks

fortyfive zeal

verbalize alongshore

oregano

fortysix

ixora

rampage onionskin

generation

fortyseven

enquiries

escargot hicktown

gothic

fortyeight

Ightham   entwined

ambient   editorships

fortynine

oeuvre

ineffectual ticktacktoe

alphabetic

fifty

young

ngwee

weepiest

staightjacket

fiftyone

onetime

mediterranean napalm

antena

garnish

omega shapes

worrisome

fiftytwo

fiftythree

reedling

linguistic

sticky

kyack

fiftyfour

ourselves   gondola

Estragon   lamb

ebonite

ardeb

fiftyfive lard

vernacular

ermine

fiftysix term negotiation

xyster

fiftyseven toneless

endoskeloton essay

ayahuasca

fiftyeight

eightvos

ostensive lips

vermicelli

fiftynine

nerve   teenybopper

velveteen   percussionist

sixty

tympan

pansexual

algebraic

iconographic

negative

sixtyone ventures

reside

deaf

sixtytwo ringleader

wondering derogate

telepathically

sixtythree

island

electrical

onchocerciasis

calculation

sixtyfour

ourang   argentine

angular   inexpressive

sixtyfive

vetchling

inglorious ruction

usufruct

amplifier

sixtysix stamp eruption

xenoblast

sixtyseven herringboned

evenly leather

lyophile

eighteenth icehouse

sixtyeight theraputic serve

sixtynine

neon

eonism antsiest

smartypants

shudder

blemish dermatoid

typeable

seventy

seventyone hilarious
nemophila usher
herald

seventytwo

womb

wombat

attic

tickseed

seventythree adversary

extra plead

trample

ouredbis

seventyfour biscotti

tip

ipsilon

seventyfive pentagram

vertebrate open

telescope

sevenntysix

xenobiotic

ticket rumour

kettledrum

seventyseven

encapsulated

arsenal

teddybears

nalorphines

elderitch

chesterfield

seventyeight larches

tubular

seventynine

ineligibility

tyre   ictus

restrict

eighty

tything

hinge

germ

ermine

eightyone

nerdy icosahedron

dyslexic rondeau

wormhole

eightytwo oleander

derelict

lictor

eightythree

reechoing

ingrown hipcheck

ownership

eightyfour

urokinases

enervation

sesquiterpene

onward

eightyfive nefarious cesspit
vespertine usances

nyla

symphony

sissy

xerosis

eightysix

eightyseven verse

entail sivers

illusive

eightyeight

eightball

allegory estimate

oryxes

eightynine

nearsighted eroticizing

tedder

ingredients

ninety

tyrannising

single

gleeful

fulmining

www.ingramcontent.com/pod-product-compliance
Lightning Source LLC
Chambersburg PA
CBHW071451070526
44578CB00001B/307
* 9 7 8 1 9 8 9 9 4 0 1 6 7 *